♥

To the glory and praise
of God the Father
and of our
Lord Jesus Christ, His Son,
and our Exalted Brother
from Whom all blessings flow!

♥

Diary of a

Mad

Caregiver

Rebecca Grace Collins

Blessings!

Rebecca Grace Collins

SCHOETTLE
PUBLISHING COMPANY

Diary of a Mad Caregiver

Published by Schoettle Publishing Company

Cover Design by Julia Marroquin

ISBN 1-56453-063-9

Printed in the United States of America

I dedicate this book to

my loving husband,

Douglas Anthony Collins

♥

And to the

precious memory of Mother,

Mary Katherine Ballard Gardner

♥

And to all my Siblings!

Thank You!

♥

God called some special people to come along side me to accomplish this great task. All of them contributed in some significant way to the completion of this book. I am deeply grateful to God, our Father, for the loving people He provided to assist me.

To Douglas: my tender warrior, husband, friend, and chief advisor. Douglas, thank you for your support every step of the way in writing this book. Without you, this book would be a dyslexic disaster. You were the first to say: *"This is the book to publish!"* Thank you, Douglas for your endless help, suggestions, editing, and loving encouragement.

Thank you, Douglas, for making it possible for us to care for Mother in our home. You have a gracious heart. I love you with all my heart.♥

To Rachel: our beloved daughter, encourager, friend, and nurse. Words can not convey our gratefulness for your skill and labor as you helped with Mother. You had to do some very hard things for her as a nurse and granddaughter. She loved you so much.

Thank you for your listening ear. I know it got difficult at times to hear my plight over and over again. Thank you for your encouraging words to us. Your Father's Day letter gave Daddy and me a glimpse of true servant-hood. We had no idea you and others were seeing us in that manner. Your words were like a refreshing stream in our wilderness. You gave us a sense of immeasurable value for our labor. Thank you Rachel and Daryl for your support! ♥

To Reuel: our son and encourager, too! Your never wavering stance on family responsibilities gave us courage to care for Mother in our home. Thank you, Reuel and Natasha for your support all the way! ♥

To Carolyn Salley: my beloved sister-in-law. You inspired me to write this book and encouraged me to believe that it could be published. Your willingness to help me get it published was what got the ball rolling. I am forever grateful for your big push to see it accomplished. Thank you for providing the help of Lynn McCraney. Thank you, Lynn, for your help was of tremendous value to the manuscript. I am thankful for your expertise. ♥

To Carolyn Brand Jackson: my beloved and special sister. You not only helped me greatly with Mother, but you were there for Mother years on end before she came to us. Thank you, Callie! You have always been there for me, too. I am grateful for your enthusiasm you showed for this book and others I have written. You have helped in endless loving ways to get this book published. The days we spent together trying to find a publisher is a treasured memory. Your determination to get it published made the dream a reality. Thank you with all my heart! ♥

To Angie Samples, who helped me so much in the planning and details of my book. You will never know how much your long talks on the phone inspired me —spiritually, emotionally, and intellectually. I am indebted to you for all that I learned from your experiences in life. Thank you, and may the Lord bless your book that you are in the process of writing. It will be a blessing to many people. ♥

To Flo Love Hernden: there would be no story to share, no book to write, no lessons learned were it not for the hand of God in your life, my dear sister, who brought Mother to us. None of us knew what God was arranging, but He had a plan concerning us far beyond caring for Mother in our home. He works all things by the council of His will. May He receive all the Glory.

Thank you, Flo, for your loving help with Mother which gave needed relief often for Doug and me to make some short trips and to attend Church on Sunday nights.

I am thankful for the countless thoughtful and kind things you and Marvin did for Mother and for us while she lived in our home. Mother loved that Marvin! Now they are together. It is with a humble heart we say, "Please receive our heartfelt thank you!" ♥

To my dear sister: Delores Kilpatrick Mikronis. Thank you for your kind words that boost me to complete the manuscript. Thank you for the early-on editing, too. Thank you for your weekly help with Mother while you lived in North Georgia. Thank you for your gifted and thoughtful entertainment for Mother while she lived with us. ♥

To Brother: better known as Chris Gardner. Thank you for spurring me on to tell the hard stuff that I needed to share for the healing of others and myself. You wouldn't let me quit until it was told —I am grateful for your insistence! You were an encouragement to me while Mother was with us, you understood my plight and you listened to my heart.

Brother, your hand crafted gifts to Mother spoke of your love and tender care for her. Thank you! ♥

To Lee Gardner, my brother, a humble servant of the Lord: Lee, I remember well how when you visited us to help with mother you lovingly washed my dishes and swept my floor.

Remember the big laugh that we had when we lost some important papers of mother's and found them in the microwave?

I'll never forget the money you slipped to me on more than one occasion as you left for home. You demonstrated your love and appreciation for me in countless tangible ways. The cards you sent with words of appreciation and thanks for caring for our mother blessed me. Thank you!

Lee, all seven of us are so glad Mother appointed you over her finances. It was a large load to carry, but you did a commendable job and in the end we were so thankful for your brilliant expertise. ♥

To Charles Gardner, a brother who cared very much for his mother and sister: Charles, we looked forward to your Saturday calls that let us know you were thinking of us. It was a blessing to Mother to hear from you each week. Thank you, Charles and Inez, for your visits and your "love gifts" to me and for Mother. You won the prize of sending Mother the most cards. Those beautiful cards came often as a steady reminder of your love for her. Thank you! ♥

To my brother, Don and his wife Lynda Gardner: Two of God's secret agents who go about helping others. God has given you a compassionate heart. Mother was one of those recipients of your watchful care.

Thank you for the Sundays we were able to attend Church because you stayed with her. Thank you for the Sunday lunches you provided during that time which were a special blessing to us. We enjoyed your visits and we are most grateful for every loving deed. ♥

To Mother's grandchildren who spent time and effort to be with her while she lived with us: there is not enough space to list you all by name and I don't want to leave one of you out! Your visits meant everything to her and were a bright ray of sunshine in her life. She loved you dearly. ♥

To Mother's only remaining sibling, Uncle Brooke Ballard: thank you and Aunt Dolly for coming with your family to cheer "Sister." Your visits, calls, and cards meant the world to her. I am so thankful you came all those miles to demonstrate your love to her. Thank you Jeannie and Mark for driving them here. God bless you as you care for your aging parents now. ♥

To my special friends: you make up the fabric of my life with your beautiful and colorful personalities that enrich my days. So it is with great pleasure to call you my beloved friends and sisters in the Lord: Audrey Roberson, Marti An Morris Windisch, Tracie Irvin, Vivian Richardson, and Barbara Photianos, you stood by me through some very hard times of caring for Mother.

Marti An, you were physically present just when I needed you in my ugliest trials. I don't know what I would have done without you then. You all were faithful in lifting me up to the Father in prayer and comforted me with your friendship. You're advice and help has been so critical in my decisions concerning the publishing of this book. Thank you!

Tracie, Barbara, and Vivian, you lovingly came to my home for lunch when I couldn't leave Mother to eat out with you. You made Mother feel special and loved when you visited with her. Your prayers helped me to accomplish God's will for my life in caring for Mother. Your friendship is a treasure, a gift from the Lord! And I am forever grateful!

Audrey, you have been around the longest as my balcony person. What would a writer do without a friend like you? You never let me lose sight of the vision of being an author. I am thankful for your wisdom and wise ideas, and council. You have constantly cheered me on. Your belief in me has kept me on track as you often said, "You can do it!" Thank you! You have cared more than I can express —you have a desire to see others succeed without a thought of "what's in it for me!" You love to encourage others and you rejoice in their accomplishments. That is a true friend.

You are not only *my* friend, but friend and an encourager to many authors. I am known among those prominent authors as "Audrey's friend." That says a lot about you, brave one.

Your dear husband, Tommy and your family have been such a blessing, too. Thank you, Tommy, for sharing your great gift of photography. You and Audrey have given our family many memories captured in unique pictures of Mother. Thank you!

♥ ♥ ♥ ♥ ♥

To the special musicians who brought the sound of music into our lives while Mother lived with us: Preacher Bethel Buchanan, the late Robert Sosebee, James Stevens, and John Gurley. Thank you for sharing your God-given talents on numerous occasions to bless my mother with your music and songs. ♥

To "Simply" Sue Falcone: I am so thankful that God crossed our paths at just the right time to give me the direction and plan He had for this book. ♥

To my dear caregivers: "Duchess" Mary Duncan, Emily Appling, Cindy Dyer, Mary Ruth Abercrombie, Cathy

McHenry, Dot Patterson, the late Gwen Nutt, Margie Harkins, Daisy Groves, Glenda Newton, Kathryn Droze, Golda Koluda, Mary Jones, Flora Mae Dockery, and Geneva Lee. Thank you for your loving care of Mother. Your presence and help with Mother gave me time to write and do other needful things. You taught me so much in the process. You were a great blessing to us as you came each week so faithfully. Thank you! ♥

To Robyn Woodmansee: a true minister of love who came to our home each Tuesday to wash and set Mother's hair. What a true labor of love you demonstrated. And we had so much fun together in the process. Thank you! ♥

To Dr. Sanders and Becky: thank you for the many home visits you made to check on Mother's health. It is a rare service in our day and time. Thank you! ♥

To the nurses and bathers of the Appalachian Home Health Care, Inc.: you lovingly cared for my Mother. We are indeed grateful for your service of love to her for us. We are glad God brought you into our home. Thank you! ♥

To Cheryl Collins: I am so very grateful for your last minute proof-reading of the manuscript. Thank you! ♥

To God: our Creator, Lord, and Savior. Thank you, Father that You love us so much that You are not willing to leave us as we are. You change our hearts through trials and pain. I am forever grateful for Your hand in my life. Thank you, Father, for allowing me to share with others Your amazing sustaining grace that carries us through any trial. ♥

Table of Content

♥

Introduction

Letter to Reader

Credits

Introduction

♥

We often think our desired haven is a place, but what joy we experience when we discover it in the Person of Jesus Christ, God's Son. The word haven is defined, according to the International Standard Bible Encyclopedia, as "A place of safety; a shelter; an asylum." I am thankful that God was a haven for me during my calling as a caregiver.

One of my heroes in the Bible is Joseph. He suffered much affliction from his brothers who were jealous of him. He was wrongly accused and sent to prison. But God used those trials to prepare Joseph for the awesome task that lay ahead of him to provide food for His people during a famine.

But God! Oh, what two precious words. It is because of His daily mercies that we are not consumed. It is He that is working out the counsel of His own will in our lives.

It was not his brothers who sent Joseph to Egypt, but God! It was not my family who orchestrated the afflictions and trials in my life, but God! How I praise Him for what He taught me in the wilderness of my affliction. I can truly say with the writer of this Psalm:

"It is good for me that I have been afflicted; that I might learn thy statutes" (Psalm 119:71).

The biblical definition of the word wilderness goes something like this: an experience that produces humility; it is where true compassion for others is born, and it is an experience not controllable by humans.

In the days of my wilderness experience, I learned to give of myself when I thought I could give no more. I learned of His sustaining grace. I learned to laugh and to value a sense of humor. I learned that singing in trials helped me to be patient. I was able to turn loose of grudges, not to hate or to be bitter. My experience taught me that Love was the answer. Watching Mother's health diminish taught me to value life. I learned the joy of being alone with Him as my true desired haven. I learned that God has a sense of humor and that humor can sustain us when in the serious business of caregiving.

The trial of caring for my mother in my own home was not all tribulation but was a real blessing in so many ways: It brought my husband and me closer to each other, but it also challenged our commitment to each other and to Mother.

It brought brothers and sisters into our home for which I had desired for years. We lived too great a distance for frequent visits. But with Mother in our home, they made the effort and visited more often. Having Mother in our home brought our family closer together after it nearly destroyed our relationships with each other. Through it all, I learned that love is the key to relationships.

Though it was not always easy for my husband, he stood by me through it all. He loved and cared for my mother right along with me. He is my hero!

I was a mad caregiver. However, as I grew in my Lord's furnace of affliction, He changed me with His love and brought me into a desired haven with Him.

It is my prayer for you, as the reader of this book, that you will let Him draw you closer to Him by His cords of love. May you be sustained by His love and mercy as your trials turn to gold. Just as God brought forth His people with joy through the wilderness, He will bring you through your wilderness experience with great joy and gladness to your desired haven with Him.

Rebecca ♥

Dear Reader,

My desire and prayer is that you make this your own diary by using the space provided for you at the end of each section.

Please pen your own thoughts, prayers, and experiences along with scripture verses that have spoken to you in your journey as a caregiver.

Blessings!

Rebecca ♥

A Desired Haven

♥

… and he brought them to their desired haven. Let them thank the Lord for his steadfast love, for his wondrous works to the children of men! Psalm107:28-31 ESV

Dreams can and do come true. Not in our way or timing, but in God's. Our dream farm was now a reality for us. We were exuberant in God's extravagant provision for us! The lovely rushing Arkaquah stream bordered our farm, and there was plenty of land for a few horses, goats, and chickens.

We were so blessed that I wanted to share this haven with others. I wrote in my prayer journal the following entry:

"Father, thank You for Your provision of a home and land. Reveal to us Your vision for this farm…Bring to our home those You want us to minister to and those who need a haven from the world. Father, develop in us the love and grace we need to fulfill Your vision for this place. Let us obey You in all Your desires for it…Truly make it a desired haven for our family, friends, and those whom You bring to us. And we will praise the Holy Name of Jesus forever." Amen.

It never occurred to me how the Lord might answer that prayer. I had my own ideas and dreams, but God had a plan. We can't tell Him what to do or who to bring. So when my mother was brought to

1

us the week of 9/11, I wondered later, *Is this who I had prayed for? ...Did I ask to be a caregiver?*

So, according to God's plan, for the next six-and-half years, Mother was in our care. We gladly gave her our bedroom and moved to the basement. The Lord had answered my prayers. We shared our home and desired haven with the person He chose to bring.

As a result of Mother living with us, many others were brought to our desired haven. Many of those God used to bless us and to grow us more into His Son's likeness.

Praise to the Lord, the Almighty...
Who o'er all things so wondrously reigneth...
Hast thou not seen
How all thy longings have been
Granted in what He ordaineth?

—Joachim Neander

♥

Thank You, Father that You give us what we need. Thank you for answering my prayer Your way. I love you!
In Jesus' Name.
Amen.
♥

My Own Thoughts and Prayers

♥

The Crucible
♥

And He shall sit as a refiner and purifier of silver:
and He shall purify the sons of Levi, and purge
them as gold and silver, that they may offer unto the
LORD an offering in righteousness.
Malachi 3:3

I Wonder

You know, Lord, how I serve You
With great emotional fervor in the limelight...
But how would I react, I wonder,
If You pointed to a basin of water
And asked me to wash the calloused feet
Of a bent and wrinkled old woman
Day after day month after month
In a room where nobody saw
And nobody knew.

— Ruth Harms Calkin

God pointed to that basin of water and
arranged for me to care for my mother in an
unexpected way. It was an unplanned visit which
stretched into years.

I'm so happy that she came. I had secretly
desired to care for her. So why was it so hard? Why
were my siblings like enemies to me? Only the Lord

knew the answers. He alone knew what lay ahead for us. I'm so glad I didn't know.

I washed my mother's feet and got her fungus-infected toes looking pretty good. I dressed her like a queen each day. She loved the attention and having me dote on her.

Like an uninvited guest, hard days stole their way into our lives. There were great trials and sickness for Mother. And I lost the vision of God's mission for me.

Consequently, I had to deal with frustration, anger, depression, and loneliness which crept into my life. But they say all these thievish troubles come as a part of caregiving.

♥

But, Lord, You sit as my Refiner.
It is painful in the heat of Your furnace.
Screaming to get out does not help.
And who cares what is happening?
You put Mother in our care. There is a job to
do and a promise to keep. You will bring me
through victoriously. Thank You, Lord!
In Jesus' Name.
Amen.
♥

6

My Own Thoughts and Prayers
♥

A Servant's Heart

♥

And the servant of the Lord must not strive;
but be gentle unto all men...
2 Timothy 2:24

Some times I wondered, *Why me? How did I get chosen for this job?* The fights and fusses I had with relatives, the persecution complex, the endless chores, and the feeling that I was the family's maid often made me ask this question.

If you, being God's child, do not have a servant's heart, He will make sure that you will have one before your caregiving days are over. God be praised for His infinite wisdom!

But the truth is that you have been hand-picked by God for this humbling task because you have a servant's heart.

The menial tasks that are necessary to the health and comfort of the loved one are hard and humbling for both caregiver and the loved one, which frequently make us fight the role of servant.

I fought the role of being a servant. Oh, it was easy enough as long as Mother appreciated what I did or when things were going smoothly with siblings. But the trials came to prove my heart.

So, what about you? Are you a caregiver who is fighting the role of a humble servant?

9

We can look to Jesus Who exemplified for us a servant's heart. On the night of the Last Supper, with His beloved disciples, Jesus used the occasion to teach a lesson in humility and selfless service. In those days, a servant washed the guests' feet, but with no servant present and no disciple assuming the role, Jesus, the Lord of all, performed the lowly task.

Jesus said:

If you know these things, blessed are you if you do them.
John 13:17 NKJV

Don't you see? You are blessed, dear caregiver! You are blessed!

♥

Thank You, Father, for Jesus. Thank You for His example for us to follow. Thank You for giving me a servant's heart. Let me please you in my service for You.
In Jesus' Name
Amen.
♥

My Own Thoughts and Prayers

♥

♥

♥

Jesus Loves Me — This I Know!

♥

Cast me not off in the time of old age;
forsake me not when my strength faileth.
Psalm 71: 9

On the fated day that Providence placed Mother in our home, she walked into our house using a four-pronged cane.

Within nine months after she came to us, she had experienced pneumonia, had all of her teeth pulled, had a pacemaker implanted, and had surgery to repair a broken hip. After that, she moved slower bent over a walker.

Now, her emotions were more frightening to her than the physical limitations of which she was experiencing. She felt unloved and rejected when she was swept out unexpectedly from her secure surroundings and brought to us, not knowing why.

Mother was to come for a short visit. I didn't even have time to collect myself or to prepare for it by taking a quick course in caregiving. For a long time, I fought resentment because the responsibility was thrown on me.

I am grateful that the Lord gave Mother and me understanding and forgiveness when we both accepted the fact that God, Who is sovereign, had placed her in my care. Now we neither one could doubt His love for us.

*And even to your old age I am He; and even
to gray hairs I will carry you! I have made and I
will bear; Even I will carry, and will deliver you.*
Isaiah 46:4 NKJV

♥

Father, we don't always understand Your plans for
us, but we can rest in the truth that You will carry
us all the way. And in the end we can proclaim,
"Jesus Loves Me —This I know!"
In Jesus' *Name.*
Amen.
♥

*Jesus loves me this I know,
for the Bible tells me so
Little ones to Him belong,
they are weak, but He is strong!
Yes, Jesus loves me.*

—*Anna B. Warner*

My Own Thoughts and Prayers
♥

♥

A Stranger

♥

I am become a stranger unto my brethren,
and an alien unto my mother's children.
Psalm 69:8

No one except the caregiver knows what it is like to take care of someone else. No matter what other family members say, they just don't know what it's like to care for someone day in and day out until they go through it themselves.

Misunderstandings and a judgmental attitude can create resentment and anger in the caregiver. I became angry, resentful, hateful, and depressed. My siblings were puzzled as to how to respond to me whenever I vented my anger on them. Consequently, they distanced themselves from me sometimes for lack of understanding of their irate sister. In fact, I didn't understand what was happening to me either at the time. I was becoming a mad woman, fit to be tied.

There are no words to explain the lonely and sad feeling I experienced when I felt estranged from my brothers and sisters when they didn't understand my anger. But God, Who is faithful, led me to an article that saved my sanity. The article explained how to cope with the stress of being a family home-care provider. It listed the warning signs of burnout.

You guessed it! Anger was listed second to irritability. The article read:

"It's common for caregivers to get easily irritated and allow their anger, frustration, and impatience to mushroom beyond normal proportions" (Caregiver Burnout [Mature Living Magazine 2004] 39).

So that's what is wrong with me, I thought. *I have caregiver burnout!*

♥

Lord, now I understand why I am so angry.
I just want a normal life like everyone else!
I feel so rejected and consumed with hate.
Turn to me and have mercy on me, for I am
alone and in deep distress. My problems
go from bad to worse. Oh, save me from
them all. Feel my pain and see my trouble.
Forgive all my sins. See how many enemies
I have, and how viciously they hate me!
Protect me! Rescue my life from them! Do
not let me be disgraced, for I trust in you.
May integrity and honesty protect me, for I
put my hope in you.
Psalm 25:16-21 NLT
Please, Lord, heal my estrange relationship
with my siblings.
For Our Elder Brother's Sake.
Amen.
♥

My Own Thoughts and Prayers
♥

♥

"Can I Call You Mother?"

♥

Who is my mother?
And who are my brethren?
And He stretched forth His hand towards His
disciples, and said,
Behold my mother and my brethren!
For whosoever shall do the will of My Father
which is in heaven,
the same is my brother, and sister, and mother.
Matthew 12: 48-50

Mother didn't know who I was this morning. Absolutely nothing I said helped her understand that her youngest daughter stood before her. Confusion continued in Mother's mind. We discussed our ages and other related things. Then she asked, "Can I call you Mother?"

My heart ached for her to be normal again, but my situation is not an isolated event. There are millions around the globe who are dealing with loved ones who have Alzheimer's, dementia, atherosclerosis, and other diseases of old age that have stolen the memory of their loved one and left them, the caregiver, to cope.

It is difficult parenting your mother or father, but if parents live long enough, the child becomes the parent as the roles are switched.

My heart ached when my mother asked me, "Are you my mother?"

21

I hate this role! I want my Mama back!

Are you in a role you hate as a caregiver?
Let's take our frustrated roles to the Lord and leave
them with Him.

♥

But, Lord, I realize it really doesn't matter
what she calls me.
What matters is that I do Your will.
And Your will for now is taking care of Mother.
Help me accept my new role as my mother's
"mother." Let me nurture her as lovingly as she did
me.

Father, I am thankful to be a part of Your Family.
Thank You for your revelation and Your wisdom,
but most of all that You love me.
Lord, You say that pure and genuine religion in the
sight of God the Father is caring for orphans and
widows in their distress (James 1:27).
That is what I want to do!
Thank You, Abba.
In Jesus' Name.
Amen.
♥

My Own Thoughts and Prayers
♥

♥

Rejoice ♪♫
♥

*This is the day the LORD hath made; we will
rejoice and be glad in it.
Psalm 118:24*

Rejoice? That's a big order for any caregiver, especially for one on her last leg or for one who is strung out to the "nth" degree!

One day Mother had repeated for 30 minutes, "O Lord, help me!" I thought she should be praying instead "O Lord, please help my daughter!"

I didn't know why she kept saying "O Lord help me." Was she hurting or was she trying to manipulate me? Did she even understand what she was saying? I knew the only thing that could save me now was to rejoice in the Lord, anyway.

I am grateful for the caregivers who came to help. They brought sunshine into our stressful lives when they arrived. One such helper bubbled with joy and encouraged Mother to repeat Psalm 118:24. She also praised the LORD and sang songs to Mother. These songs made our spirits rise above the banalities of the job.

Another jovial helper sang "You Are My Sunshine," which was Mother's favorite song. She managed to rouse Mother to sing …"all around the water tank waiting for a train."

God gives us music to lift our spirits when they drag the ground. He gives us songs in the dark nights of our lives.

King David wrote in Psalms 32:7, "Thou art my hiding place; Thou shalt compass me about with songs of deliverance. Selah." Selah means to stop and think about it.

Just think! God can be our hiding place from trouble if we come under His wing of protection. He will surround us with songs of deliverance from depression, despair, and from drowning in our own self-pity. Praise His Name!

Truly, I can say, "This is the day the LORD hath made; I will rejoice and be glad in it! I will be happy today!"

♥

Father, thank You for songs of deliverance.
In Jesus' Name.
Amen.
♥

My Own Thoughts and Prayers
♥

♥

Bowels of Mercy

♥

Put on therefore,
as the elect of God,
holy and beloved, bowels of mercy.
Colossians 3:12

"O no! Not again!" Sound familiar? At least, these were my thoughts when Mother had frequent accidents!

Bowel movements can be one of the most frustrating tasks there is for a caregiver. They're serious business because a fecal impaction can lead to obstruction, which in turn can lead to death. However, the "runs" can keep the caregiver hopping and crying out to the Lord.

The daily chores: wiping bottoms, emptying and cleaning the bedside toilet, changing their clothes and pull-ups, and scrubbing the floor from an accident will stretch the emotions and patience of any saint!

But my heart broke, as she cried from the embarrassment and humiliation of a bowel accident. When that happened, I comforted her in my arms and reassured her of the great value her life was to me and others.

However, some days after changing her for the fifth time, it took a lot of self-control and a determined smile to change her one more time.

The phrase, "Bowels of mercy," mentioned in the above scripture are necessary tools for us to deal with the day-to-day consequences of caregiving. This is the heart of compassion. We can glorify the Lord in all that we do when we let our hearts practice the thoughts of A. W. Tozer:

"My daily labors can be performed
as acts of worship acceptable to God
by Christ Jesus."

♥

Thank you, Father, for giving me Your compassion — bowels of mercy. Help me be patient when Mother has an accident. Let it be an act of worship of You.

She deserves my labor of love, for she changed her share of diapers for me and the other eight children, too.

Thank You for extending Your love even when we mess up in life. Thank You for Your bowels of mercy and compassion. I love You, Lord.
In Jesus' Sweet Name.
Amen.
♥

My Own Thoughts and Prayers
♥

♥

Who's House?

♥

Use hospitality one to another
without grudging.
1Peter 4:9

When God sent Mother to us in order that we might minister to her, it called for the help of many other devoted hands. God was always faithful to provide the helpers we needed. Even though not all of them were what I had anticipated, somehow they met the needs at the time. I am so grateful to each of them. They taught me so much.

It was intensely frustrating for me at times to deal with the different personalities. However, one of the greatest challenges was the denial of privacy.

Dying daily to the desire for privacy became paramount. It wasn't easy for me to share our home, including, my kitchen, my bathroom, and my couch. Sharing the time with Mother with someone else present was not always easy, either. However, we discovered we couldn't accomplish this alone. The need for help was so crucial!

Therefore, it was necessary to have other caregivers, doctors, nurses, bathers, visitors, and insurance interviewers to help me with Mother's health.

We kept a daily log of Mother's medicines, and other important data concerning her care. One evening while sitting with Mother, I wrote some of my frustrations in the back of the logbook. I thought no one would look in the back! I just had to vent my feelings —somewhere. But soon the night nurse found me out and wrote the following response:

"Rebecca, I know I entered into your private world when I read your notes. I'm sorry! I had to read almost all of it thru tears. You can feel your compassion and love in the words…It's all so clear now. We both needed each other…" *Mary Ruth*

Could these be the people I asked God to bring to our desired haven? Lord, how could I have been so selfish?

♥

Father, forgive my attitude and take away any guilt in my heart so I can show hospitality without a grudge. Thank You for the helpers who care so lovingly for mother and who give me free time to do other things.

But, Father, I know You understand because a throng of people surrounded Your Son as He walked this earth. He needed to get away, too.

Make our home a haven for others, a place of peace and love for all who come through its doors. Bring to our home whoever You desire.

In Jesus' Name.
Amen
♥

My Own Thoughts and Prayers
♥

♥

Checking Out of Here!

♥

Your eyes saw my unformed substance,
and in Your book all the days [of my life]
were written before ever they took shape,
when as yet there was none of them.
Psalm 139:16 AMP

One particular morning, my ninety-seven-year-old mother woke up with one thing on her mind. As she threw back the covers and struggled to get up, she said "I've got to get dressed and check out of here to go home. There's a plan of what I am to do," she said as she surveyed her bed. "It's written down here somewhere." Even in her confusion, she felt the pull of heaven on her soul.

Mother's words, "I've got to check out of here," brought to my mind the above scripture that all our days were written in God's Book before we were conceived. The Bible says there's "A time to be born and a time to die..." Ecclesiastes 3:2.

Mother's soul was restless as she yearned for heaven —her real home.

"How can I get out of here?" she asks in desperation. Though she tried to leave, she was still bound to her aging body.

One day Mother asked me what I thought heaven would be like. After she had listened to my description, she replied, "Well, why would we want to stay down here any longer?" Heaven is indeed a wonderful place!

As it is written:

Eye hath not seen, nor ear heard, neither have entered into the heart of man, the things which God hath prepared for them that love Him.
I Corinthians 2: 9

♥

Father, Maker of Heaven and earth and Lord of all, it is a comfort to know that all of our days and our "check-out times" are written down in Your book. Thank You for the promise of the glories of Heaven for Your children when we "check out of here." Help mother to be patient until You come to take her home with You.
In the Name of Jesus.
Amen.
♥

My Own Thoughts and Prayers
♥

♥

Help! Somebody!
Is It All Right to Feel This Way?
♥

Let not your heart be troubled:
ye believe in God,
believe also in Me.
John 14:1

If we were honest with ourselves, we would admit that there are times when we didn't want the responsibility of caregiving.

I keep asking the LORD to do a work in me as if I am the one holding Mother back from Glory. I am so tired. Sometimes I feel I can't help her to the toilet one more time. I can't stand to hear her cry out, "Oh, Lord, help me!". I can't drag myself out of bed at 2 a.m. another time. Nor do I feel I can climb the stairs half asleep again.

Then, guilt comes crushing in like a raging river from Mother and myself. *It's bad to feel this way*, I think to myself. I know that God's Word says to honor your parents, but what if you are too tired to think or too exhausted to pray?

The song, an old African-American spiritual, expresses my feelings precisely:

Nobody knows de trouble I've seen
Nobody knows de trouble but Jesus
Nobody knows de trouble I've seen
Glory Hallelujah!

41

Sometimes I'm up, sometimes I'm down
Oh, yes, Lord
Sometimes I'm almost to de ground'
Oh, yes, Lord.

Glory Hallelujah!

Even though, we are up and down with our feelings and are troubled on every side, a few words of encouragement can help to level out these emotions. I received that kind of encouragement in a Christmas card that read:

"You will never know the full gratitude we feel for your love and care of Mother..."

—Brother

♥

Jesus, thank You that You have seen my trouble, and that You send encouragement through a brother or a sister. Thank You for the strength to finish the task You have given me to do. Thank You for understanding how I feel. Thank You for your forgiveness when I want to throw my hands up and quit! Let not my heart be troubled.
I love You.
In Jesus' Name.
Amen.
♥

My Own Thoughts and Prayers
♥

♥

Do You Have a Room?

♥

Return to your rest, O my soul,
For the LORD has dealt bountifully with you.
Psalm 116:7 NKJV

"It's getting too much for me again," I told my husband one exasperating day. "I need time to get away." I was tired and my temper was getting short, and of course, my husband had already noticed that.

It had been a few years since we had rafted the Nantahala River. Did we have the confidence to do it again? My husband made plans with one of my sisters to care for Mother while we were gone to the Carolina Mountains.

After rafting, we decided to wear our wet clothes and change in the motel only a few miles away. On our way, my husband said, "Let's stop by the Hawkesdene House Bed and Breakfast and see if they have a room for us". "No!" I protested. "You know that they stay booked-up months in advance." We knew that because we had gone by before and met the owners. We had walked on their lovely grounds and longed to stay there someday.

As we drove to the front door, the inn keeper stepped out of the house. I was so embarrassed that I could have melted into the car seat. *What would she think?*

"Do you have a room?" my husband asked. "I have a room if your name is Doug Collins." I couldn't believe my ears. He had made reservations to surprise me! Tears of joy flowed down my astonished face.

We enjoyed the best room in the house: A refreshing Jacuzzi, a rushing mountain stream in the backyard, and a gourmet breakfast the next morning.

Every caregiver needs a getaway haven and I had been given mine. Thank You, Lord.

♥

Thank You, Father, for a husband who likes to surprise me with good things. Thank You for refreshing and renewing my spirit. I now know You have many blessings in store for Your children who look to You for help and believe in Your faithfulness. Praise Your Holy Name!
Amen.
♥

My Own Thoughts and Prayers
♥

♥

Goodness and Mercy

♥

Surely goodness and mercy
shall follow me
all the days of my life...
Psalm 23:6a

Earlier in my mother's stay with us, she sang along with me the song, "Surely Goodness and Mercy." She clung to the promises of God. In the midst of Mother's pain and confusion, she still knew His goodness would never fail her.

On the contrary, there were times for me when it was not so easy to trust in God's goodness. Caring for an elderly parent can cause depression and hopelessness in the caregiver. I often wondered: *How long can I hold out? How old will I be when she goes home to be with the Lord? Will I be too old to enjoy the life I have left?* As my life was quickly passing by, I knew that these were my good years before I, too, would need help.

Such thoughts can push the panic button or cause a feeling of being trapped. Worst of all, they can cause a feeling of pure hopelessness about the future. However though, none of us are promised a tomorrow.

If I had known the brevity of Mother's days, then I would not have worried and fretted, but we are not privy to that information.

49

Like Mother, I needed to trust the Lord with my future. His Word says "...my times are in Thy hands" (Psalm 31:15). I will rest in that promise. He has all things under control and His timing.

♥

Father, give me strength and faith to trust You with Mother's future and mine. Give me contentment where You have placed me to serve You. I cling to Your promises. We will sing and believe, as David did, that goodness and mercy will follow us all the days of our lives.

In Jesus' Name.

Amen.

♥

Stayed upon Jehovah, Hearts are fully blest-finding, as He promised, Perfect peace and rest.

—Havergal

My Own Thoughts and Prayers
♥

Bent Out of Shape!

♥

I will go before you,
and make the crooked places straight...
Isaiah 45:2

Bent, twisted, and tied in a knot! That is how I was feeling one Sunday afternoon in March. I thought, *There is so much more to this caregiving than I ever thought it would require. It asks for more than I can give. How can I go on and on with the conflicts and burdens I have been dealt? My life and relationships were out of kilter.*

But God sent encouragement through His Word promising that He would go before me and make everything bent out of shape in my life into straight paths for my feet if I would follow Him and His path for my life.

Therefore, I could trust that He would take my crooked thoughts, motives, relationships, and even my crooked teeth now in braces, and make them pleasing. He would give me strength to endure. I could believe His Word to me.

You can believe His Word, too. He has the power to do all things. He can straighten what is bent out of shape in your life, and He will be glorified when you let Him.

And let us not be weary in well doing: for in due season we shall reap, (things straightened) if we faint not.
Galatians 6:9

Lord, bend this stubborn
will of mine
until it conforms to
Your Design.
—rgc

♥

Father, I needed those words of encouragement that I will not be ashamed, but that you will go before me in all I do. I have wanted to give up on taking care of Mother, give up writing my books and getting them published, and I am ready to get these braces removed! Why did I wait so late in life to have my teeth straightened? There are other things too numerous to relate, but You know all about them. Thank You that You are taking care of all my needs while You go before me making the crooked places straight. I trust Your everlasting love.
In Jesus' Name.
Amen.
♥

54

My Own Thoughts and Prayers
♥

Comfort the Feebleminded

♥

Now we exhort you, brethren...
comfort the feebleminded, support the weak,
be patient toward all men.
I Thessalonians 5:14

An American pioneer rocket scientist, Dr. Robert H. Goddard, said:

"Resolve to be tender with the young, compassionate with the aged, sympathetic with the striving, and tolerant with the weak and the wrong. Sometime in life you will have been all of these."

But even with that thought, it takes the patience of Job to care for someone day in and day out, doesn't it?

Furthermore, all that we can do to help our loved ones is to comfort them, support them with our presence, and develop patience with their needs. Paul reminds us in the Scriptures to exhibit these attributes because they do not come naturally. We depend on the Lord to develop them in us.

Mother wanted and needed someone to hold her hand almost all the time. She was afraid to be left alone. It felt confining to be there every minute. Sometimes she seemed demanding, but she just needed love and reassurance much like a child full of fear.

Old age is not a disease. It is a stage of life, a reverting to the childhood days in many ways. The

57

elderly are helpless and dependent on others like a little child.

The song "Jesus, Lover of My Soul" written by Charles Wesley expresses the cry of the elderly:

Other refuge, have I none;
Hangs my helpless soul on Thee;
Leave, oh, leave me not alone.
Still support and comfort me.
All my trust on Thee is stayed,
all my help from Thee I bring;
cover my defenseless head
with the shadow of Thy wing.

♥

Lord, thank You for Your presence which comforts me and helps me comfort Mother. Help me support her in her weak and helpless condition, remembering that one day I may be old, too, with needs like hers.
For Jesus' Sake.
Amen.
♥

58

My Own Thoughts and Prayers
♥

♥

A Merry Heart

♥

A merry heart doeth good like a medicine:
but a broken spirit drieth the
bones.
Proverbs 17:22

Did you know a sense of humor can make a person healthier? Mother's sense of humor was delightful and refreshing to all who knew her! (Maybe that's why she lived so long.) She was quick with her wit giving those who served her a real chuckle or peals of laughter.

It is a scientific fact that laughter will do wonders for the body. Many physicians have studied it and found that laughter gives almost every organ in. the body a great workout. It exercises muscles in the face, arms, legs and the diaphragm. Laughter relieves tension and depression and aids digestion. Laughter also releases hormones that stimulate the heart and breathing which causes the arteries to contract and then relax.

The number one beneficial effect of laughter is the fact that it increases the body's production of endorphins. Endorphins are natural painkillers for the body. Therefore, endorphins benefit both the patient and the caregivers.

On one particular morning Mother had slept later than usual. Upon waking, she flung the covers back, hung her legs off the side of the bed, and said,

"I guess I better get up and let my bed air out. If I don't, I'll be glued to this bed!"

♥

Thank you, Father, for laughter. Thank You
for the reminder in Your word that
"… he that is of a merry heart hath a
continual feast" (Proverbs 151:15).

Thank you for laughter's healing power.
Thank You for Your wonderful design to heal and
help us cope.

Thank You for Mother's quick wit and
humor. Thank You for the feast of laughter with her.
Help me to look on the funny side of life as I care
for my sweet mother.
In Jesus' Name.
Amen.
♥

My Own Thoughts and Prayers
♥

♥

64

Rest for the Weary
♥

Come unto me,
all ye that labour and are heavy laden,
and I will give you rest.
Take my yoke upon you, and learn of me;
for I am meek and lowly in heart:
and ye shall find rest unto your souls.
For my yoke is easy,
and my burden is light.
Matthew 11:28-30

Most caregivers may not realize that it is ok to go out into the backyard, or into the basement, or into the woods to scream! However, the neighbors might need to know that they can expect it from time to time so they won't call the police.

In any case, caregivers do get overwhelmed by the heavy responsibilities of caring for an elderly parent, a loved one with Alzheimer's disease, or someone with a physical handicap.We often want to release our emotions with a loud and prolong scream! AND IT'S OK!

The constant, continuous, laborious, and never-ending responsibility of caring for a loved one takes super strength and power that does come naturally. Add in family problems, and one may think, *what's the use? I might as well give up!*

Instead of giving up, we can go to the Rock of our salvation and find strength and rest for our weary souls.

Hear my cry, O God; attend unto my prayer.
From the end of the earth will I cry unto Thee,
when my heart is overwhelmed:
lead me to that rock that is higher than I.
For Thou hast been a shelter for me,
and a strong tower from the enemy.
Psalm 61:1-3

…As thy days so, shall thy strength be.
Deuteronomy 33:25

♥

Father, Thank You that we can scream and vent our emotions when life is too overwhelming for us. Thank You for being our Rock and Fortress where we can find rest for our weary souls.
In Jesus' Name.
Amen.
♥

My Own Thoughts and Prayers
♥

♥

Others Are Watching!

♥

In the same way, let your light so shine before others, so that they would see your good works and give glory to your Father who is in heaven.
Matthew 5:16 NIV

Often we become so caught up in the pressures of caregiving that we forget we have an audience of children, friends, siblings, helpers, store attendants, doctors, nurses, bathers, and the list goes even to "the cloud of witnesses" (Hebrews 12:10) that surround us.

We were unaware of the message on the billboard of our lives until our daughter sent her dad this email for Father's Day:

"Dear Daddy,

Since a man shall leave his father and mother and become one flesh with his wife, I write this to both you and mother.

Today, I want to give glory to our Father for the light of good works shining so brightly in your lives. All my life I have basked in its warmth, but especially now. Worldly thinking would suggest you have come to a time of retirement from toil and work. Yet God has providentially asked more of you both than ever before.

69

I glorify God today for every time you have lifted, comforted, washed, cleaned, carried, assisted, reoriented, soothed, assured, bandaged, fed, wiped, listened to, answered the same question, tucked-in, covered-up, overlooked, prayed for, dressed, transferred, gone without_____, prepared food for, given a cup of cold water, and placed someone else's need above your own.

HIS worth is more clear and glorious because of your selfless and sacrificial giving, loving, and caring. Your life is NOT being wasted although it is being poured out as a drink offering. God created us for His glory (Isaiah 43:6-7). Thank you for living for His glory and warming our lives with your good works. Soli Deo Gloria!

Your grateful daughter,

Rachel"

♥

Father, make us mindful that this is not just about us, but for others, too, who may be watching.
Thank you, Father
for encouragement in this awesome task.
May You receive all the glory!
In Jesus' Precious Name.
Amen.

♥

My Own Thoughts and Prayers
♥

His Eye Is On the Sparrow
♥

Are not five sparrows sold for two farthings, and
not one of them is forgotten before God?
But even the very hairs of your
head are all numbered. Fear not therefore:
ye are of more value than many sparrows.
Luke 12:6

"When words fail, Music speaks."

—Hans Christian Anderson

There were times when I was unable to say anything that brought comfort to Mother's troubled heart. That's when music soothed and calmed her fears. The Bible tells us that before David became king of Israel, he knew how music could soothe and calm a troubled heart when he played his harp in the presence of King Saul.

The one song that always lifted Mother's troubled spirit and inspired her to sing along with me was: "His Eye Is On the Sparrow."

Isn't it wonderful to realize that God never takes His eyes off of us. He values us so much that He knows each hair on our head and numbers them. Since He also notices when a sparrow falls to the ground, will He not take care of us and see to every detail of our lives?

It seems easy enough to trust God when things are going well, but when circumstances change, and fear creeps into one's life —now, that's another thing. But His eye is always on us. Praise the Lord.

Why should I feel discourage?
Why should the shadow come?
Why should my heart be lonely,
and lone for heaven and home?
When Jesus is my portion,
My constant friend is He:
His eye is on the sparrow
...and I know He watches me.

—*Ethel Waters*

♥

Father, I know You are watching over Mother intently and You are watching how I care for her. Sometimes I'm not as patient and loving as you are, but remind me that You are caring for us both and are watching us with great love.
In Jesus' Name.
Amen
♥

74

My Own Thoughts and Prayers
♥

Sundowner's Syndrome

♥

*...I will fear no evil: for Thou art with me; Thy rod
and Thy staff they comfort me.*
Psalm 23:4

As the sun sets in the late afternoon and
evening, a black, eerie cloud settles over many of
the elderly. They become edgy, irritable, scared,
paranoid, nervous, and depressed. It seems that their
spirits sink with the setting sun.

Nurses told us that such symptoms happen
daily in nursing homes. They call this condition in
the elderly "Sundowner's Syndrome," which is
characterized by fear, forgetfulness, confusion, and
disorientation.

"Lord, please take care of me!" Mother
prayed this prayer each evening as fear gripped her
soul. We engaged in a spiritual battle by singing
hymns, praying and reading the Word.

At this time, I sang a song to her that she
had often sung when I was a young girl. She filled
our home with music from the lyrics of the song:
God Will Take Care of You!

Be not dismayed whatever betide,
God will take care of you;
Beneath His wings of love abide,
God will take care of you.
No matter what may be the test,

God will take care of you;
Lean, weary one, upon His breast,
God will take care of you;
Refrain:
God will take care of you,
Thro' every day, o'er all the way;
He will take care of you,
God will take care of you.

— Civilla D. Martin

♥

Father, help us to cope during this time of Sundowner's, a time we dread each day. Help us to lean upon Your Word, Your rod, and Your staff to comfort us. We will fear no evil, for Thou art with us.

Thank You that we can cast all our fears upon You because You never cease to care for us.

In Jesus' Name.

Amen.

♥

My Own Thoughts and Prayers

♥

♥

Twice a Child

♥

Verily I say unto you, Except ye be converted,
and become as little children, ye shall not enter into
the kingdom of heaven. Whosoever therefore shall
humble himself as this little child, the same is
greatest in the kingdom of heaven.
And whosoever shall receive one such little child in
my name, receiveth Me.
Matthew 18:3-5

"When will Mother and Daddy come to get me? I wanted to stay, but I didn't know I was going to feel so bad," Mother asked me one day. Elderly parents turn into innocent little children again and sometimes angry, unmanageable children.

Just like a little child she asked, "Have you seen my Mother and Daddy?"

My heart would ache as she asked me this question. She was like a little child lost from her parents.

There is an old saying that rings true: "Once a man, twice a child." Not only did I have to do almost everything for her, but she also reversed the roles. I became the parent, and she became my child. It was a humbling experience for Mother and for me.

81

We all are someone's child, anyway. But I want to
be known as a child of the King!

I'm a child of the King,
A child of the King,
With Jesus my Savior
I'm a child of the King.

—*Harriet E. Burell*

♥

Father, thank You for making me Your child.
Help me act like Your child. I want to please You in
caring for my mother. You tell us in Your Word
that we all need to humble ourselves and become as
little children in our hearts. I want to be like Jesus,
who humbled Himself and took on the form of a
servant.

I am the Mother now, comforting, directing,
teaching and listening. Give me strength to do this
humbling task. Help me to please You, Father, in
how I care for my mother who is now a child once
again.
In the Savior's Name, Jesus.
Amen.
♥

My Own Thoughts and Prayers

♥

♥

A Grateful Heart

♥

In everything give thanks: for this is the will of
God in Christ Jesus concerning you.
I Thessalonians 5: 18

"God has two dwellings; one in heaven, and
the other in a meek and thankful heart."

— Izaak Walton

Nancy Leigh De Moss expressed the results
of giving thanks in this way: "When we choose the
pathway of worship and giving thanks, especially in
the midst of difficult circumstances, there is a
fragrance, a radiance that issues forth out of our
lives to bless the Lord and others." I don't know
about you, but I want to "smell good" to the Lord
and to others!

Sometimes while serving the Lord as a
caregiver, our hearts get weighed down to the
ground. However, giving thanks to the Lord for His
goodness will make our load lighter and our hearts
joyful.

How delighted God must have been to hear
Fanny Crosby say, "It seemed intended by the
blessed Providence of God that I should be blind all
my life, and I thank Him for the dispensation."
Because Fanny cultivated a grateful heart instead of
resenting her station in life, she blessed the world
with 8,000 songs. What a sweet-smelling fragrance
she was to the Lord. As we caregivers develop a

spirit of thanksgiving, we can be a great blessing to God and also to our loved ones, too.

To God be the glory great things He has done...Come to the Father thru Jesus the Son, and give Him the glory great things He hath done.

—Fanny Crosby

♥

Father, as we go about our days and nights of caregiving, help us to honor You with our thoughts of gratitude, thereby we will fulfill the command in Colossians 3:17:

And whatsoever ye do in word or deed, do all in the name of the Lord Jesus, giving thanks to God and the Father by Him.

Let us remember that: "It is a good thing to give thanks unto the LORD, and to sing praises unto Thy name, most High: To shew forth Thy lovingkindness in the morning and Thy faithfulness every night" (Psalm 92:1-2).
In my Savior's Name.
Amen.
♥

My Own Thoughts and Prayers
♥

When Wounds Become Windows
♥

He healeth the broken in heart
and bindeth up their wounds.
Psalm 147:3

When wounds become windows clearer than glass
and we finally see through the pain. That all of our
suffering when counted at last could never amount
to our gain. Til our wounds become windows and
we see through the pain.

—Bob Kilpatrick

Scores of people who are taking care of their parents have unresolved emotions and problems that have been carried over from their childhood. These emotional problems cloud our view of reality even in adulthood.

While growing up, I could not express my true thoughts to Mother. I camouflaged them with a smile while seething with anger inside.

Suppressed anger is said to be the most toxic and dangerous emotion of them all. It caused severe internal problems for me as a young girl. I suffered greatly in body and spirit.

While Mother lived with me, the submerged emotions deep in my spirit surfaced. I thought I was losing my mind as the anger showed it ugly head. *Where was all this anger coming from?* I wondered. I finally faced my emotions head-on. Although, it

was a painful ordeal to go through, God helped me
sort out my feelings, and His grace enabled me to
be transparent with my mother at last.

Maybe you are carrying some hurts from
your childhood, also. Maybe you are experiencing
anger, too. Jesus came to deliver us from evil. He
came to heal the brokenhearted and to bind up our
wounds.

For I will restore health unto thee, and I will heal
thee of thy wounds, saith the Lord...
Jeremiah 30:17

♥

Thank You, Father, for Your healing power. Thank
You for letting me see Your rich mercies and grace
through the pain.
In Jesus' Precious Name.
Amen.

♥

My Own Thoughts and Prayers
♥

Lord, Help Me Say It Right!

♥

Let the words of my mouth,
and the meditation of my heart,
be acceptable in Thy sight,
O LORD,
my strength, and my redeemer.
Psalm 19:14

If you have siblings, then you know that the sibling relationship is one of the most challenging in life. These relationships are especially challenging when we find ourselves captives of old childhood behavior patterns while we are caring for an elderly parent.

Our words to each other can cause pain, and we are surprised many times when the other person is hurt by something we innocently say. Sometimes we are hurt by their words. Often what one says and what the other hears is not the same thing. *For the ear tests words as the palate tastes food (Job 34:3ESV).*

My ears tested every word I heard from my siblings. I needed encouragement, not advice. Often the message got distorted somewhere between my ears and my brain. Maybe it was their tone of voice, or maybe it was bad timing. Or maybe it was me. The condition of my heart had a lot to do with my reaction to what they said. As the Word says,

...Let everything you say be

93

good and helpful, so that your words will be an
encouragement to those who hear them.
Ephesians 4:29 NLT

Proverbs 16: 24 says:

Pleasant words are as an honeycomb,
sweet to the soul,
and health to the bones.

Now, I don't know about you, but I want healthy bones!

♥

Father, let our words be pleasing to You and let them edify others and be pleasant to the ears of the hearers. Let the meditations of our hearts be acceptable in Your sight.

Lord, help us not to let childhood rivalries spill over into our adult lives with angry words. Help us to understand each other's heart and listen for the real message. I want my siblings to understand me. Mostly, I need to understand them and what they are saying. I know they really want to help. Enable me to let them.

In Our Elder Brother's Name, Jesus.
Amen.
♥

My Own Thoughts and Prayers
♥

♥

The Great Escape

♥

And I said, Oh that I had wings like a dove!
for then would I fly away, and be at rest.
Psalm 55:6

Escape? Fly away? Yes! Let's be honest.
We caregivers dream of escaping our circumstances,
don't we? We dream of how it used to be, and we
think of how it could be. But the truth is, we are
most miserable people if we don't accept our
circumstances.

The late Jim Elliot, missionary to the Auca
Indians and martyr for Jesus, wrote in his diary in
1950:

"Wherever you are, be all there. Live to the
hilt every situation you believe to be the will of
God."

That's very good advice, and yet we still
want to escape our situation. I thought many times I
might have to die as a result of caring for mother. I
didn't think that I was going to make it physically
and emotionally. Now, that would be escaping all
right.

I remember moments when I knew I would
lay down my life, if necessary, for my mother. I
didn't want to give up caring for her, even if it cost
me my life.

But, "living to the hilt" is not easy, for it means we are enjoying God's will for our lives and not seeking ways to escape like my husband and I did.

So when I want to fly away, I sing:

Hide me, when the storm is raging
O'er life's troubled sea;
Like a dove on ocean's billows,
O let me fly to Thee.

— *Fanny Crosby*

♥

When I fly to You, Father,
I can be all there for my loved one
and live life to the hilt.
Thank You!
Amen.

♥

My Own Thoughts and Prayers
♥

♥

Never Alone
♥

...I am like a pelican of the wilderness: I am like an owl of the desert. I watch, and am as a sparrow alone upon the house top.
Psalm 102: 6-7

My neighbor, who was an only child, cared for her mother alone. She shared with me that she didn't feel alone because she never knew what it was like to have a brother or sister to share the load.

Even though I had seven siblings, and there were over fifty million caregivers in the United States, I still felt a degree of loneliness while caring for my mother.

However though, there were many times my sisters and brothers came to my rescue. They came when my husband and I needed to take a few days off, or when Doug had to go to a medical meeting out of town, or when we went to church. I was so grateful for each time they helped, but they could go home after they helped me. That's when I felt the loneliest.

Although the responsibility for the care of Mother was not really totally mine, my brothers and sisters were limited in what they could do to help me. If Mother had been in her own home, they would have felt more relaxed in helping care for her.

Nonetheless, whenever I felt alone like the sparrow on the roof top, I found solace in God's

Word, and I found comfort in songs such as Ludie D. Pickett's "Never Alone."

When in affliction's valley
I'm treading the road of care,
My Savior helps me to carry
My cross when heavy to bear,
Though all around me is darkness,
Earthly joys all flown;
My Savior whispers His promise,
'I never will leave thee alone.'
No, never alone, No, never alone,
He promised never to leave me,
Never to leave me alone.

Therefore, we can have faith in God when our pathway is lonely. He knows the way in which we have to go. He watches over His children, therefore, we may be lonely, but we are never alone.

♥

Father, how comforting to know that
The Lord of hosts is with us;
the God of Jacob is our refuge. Selah.
Psalm 46:11

♥

My Own Thoughts and Prayers

♥

The Fellowship of His Sufferings
♥

In all their affliction
He was afflicted...
Isaiah 63:9

What a comfort to know that God feels our afflictions and cries with us. We can feel His presence with us in our misery, distress, hardship, trial, oppression, calamity, and anguish. He is in it with us all the way, feeling it and yet holding us up.

He even stores our tears in a bottle in heaven, and they are written about in His book (Psalm 56:8). Aren't you glad He doesn't say, "Oh, here comes 'cry baby' again," when we cry out to Him?

But instead, He feels our pain, cries with us, and keeps our tears in special jars. Doesn't that make you wonder just how big those bottles must be when He stores the tears of caregivers?

The author of Hebrews tells us:

For we have not an high priest which can not be
touched with the feeling of our infirmities; but was
in all points tempted like as we are, yet without sin.
Hebrews 4:15

Suffering has been a part of life since the fall of man. God will be there for us, when we call upon Him.

105

Bill Schakat, our teaching elder at our church states it so clearly:

"He is available to help us in our time of need, because He has been raised from the dead and ever lives to make intercession for His people. He is 'waiting' until we call. He is working His will in the midst of our suffering. He works all things out for our good and His glory."

Let us therefore come boldly unto the throne of grace, that we might obtain mercy, and find grace to help in time of need.
Hebrews 4:16

♥

Thank You, Father, for the fellowship of suffering we experience with You as we labor in this task together.
Father, thank You for feeling our pain when we hurt. It is hard for us to understand love like Yours that gathers up our trickling tears when we cry out to You. Thank You for help in our time of need. Give us the faith to come boldly to Your throne of grace.
In The Lovely Name of Jesus.
Amen.
♥

My Own Thoughts and Prayers

♥

♥

♥

Why is There Suffering?
♥

Wherefore let them that suffer according to the will of God commit the keeping of their souls to him in well doing as unto a faithful Creator.
I Peter 4:19

Have you ever wondered why there is suffering in the world? I have so wondered. Here are a few things to ponder. God made a perfect world without sin, sickness, suffering or pain. Adam and Eve, whom God created on the sixth day, chose not to believe God's word and sinned through disobedience. That's when sin, suffering, and death entered into God's perfect world.

Wherefore, as by one man sin entered into the world, and death by sin...
Romans 5:12.

The Bible tells us clearly in 2 Corinthians 1:3&4 that suffering teaches us how to comfort others, so that we might be a comfort to others who are going through situations similar to those we have been through.

Blessed be God, even the Father of our Lord Jesus Christ, the Father of mercies, and the God of all comfort; Who comforteth us in all our tribulation, that we may be able to comfort them which are in any trouble, by the comfort wherewith we ourselves are comforted of God.

But praise God there is a new day coming soon. His Word tells us in Revelation 21:4 that:

... God shall wipe away all tears from their eyes; and there shall be no more death, neither sorrow, nor crying neither shall there be any more pain: for the former things are passed away.

♥

Thank You, Lord, for comforting us in order that we may comfort others. Thank You for the promise of a new world to come with no more suffering, and no more pain.
In Jesus' Name.
Amen.
♥

My Own Thoughts and Prayers

♥

Never Forgotten

♥

…yea, they may forget,
yet will I not forget thee…
Isaiah 49:15

It is very easy to feel abandon and forgotten when you are confined with the task of taking care of someone else. Especially, when others, family or friends, eat out together and you have to stay home with the loved one.

Furthermore, there were times in the years Mother was with us that I felt especially abandoned as my siblings pulled out of our driveway to go home after a family gathering. I stood on the steps waving as my heart sank into despair. The weight of the responsibility was felt on our shoulders again. I wanted to scream: "Wait! Don't leave me. Please come back. I need you! Please stay and help!" But they had burdens to bear, promises to keep, and work to be done. It wasn't their fault I felt abandoned.

Perhaps you have felt that way, too, when you had to carry the responsibility of your loved one alone while others in your family went about their own lives. The good news is that we have not been forgotten by God! Listen to what God's word says to comfort us:

Can a woman forget her nursing child, and have no
compassion on the son of her womb? Even these
may forget, but I will not forget you.
Isaiah 49:15 NKJV

If we are a part of His Family, He says:

See, I have inscribed you
on the palms of My hands;
your walls are continually before Me.
Isaiah 49:16 NKJV

♥

Father, may we grasp the depth of Your love for us:
A love that never forgets or abandons.
A love that comforts and strengthens.
A love that gave Your only Son for Your people.
Thank You for Your everlasting love.
Amen.
♥

My Own Thoughts and Prayers

♥

♥

How Sweet It Is!

♥

How wonderful, how beautiful,
when brothers and sisters get along!
It's like costly anointing oil
Flowing down head and beard,
Flowing down Aaron's beard,
Flowing down the collar of his priestly robes.
It's like the dew on Mount Hermon
Flowing down the slopes of Zion.
Yes, that's where God commands the blessing,
Ordains eternal life.
Psalm 133:1-3 The Message

What a lovely picture of unity in the family that the Psalmist paints for us in these verses. How sweet unity can be among brethren.

How sweet it is… but have you ever wished that you could pick another family? Maybe on a few occasions I have, but that precious gift is not ours to choose because it is given and chosen for us by God.

He puts us in a particular family where each individual has different gifts, abilities, and talents that complement each other.

The heavy responsibility of caregiving may crowd this truth out and cause the caregiver to miss this important aspect. Shared responsibilities can make the caregiver's load much lighter.

Let's look earnestly for our siblings special abilities and put them to work, for the family was

117

God's idea. And He smiles when we pull together. Besides, it glorifies Him as we do.

Got any family members you need to put to work? They may be by the phone waiting for your call right now.

There is no doubt that it is around the family and the home that all the greatest virtues, the most dominating virtues of human society, are created, strengthened and maintained.

—Winston Churchill

♥

Father, give us a life running over with the oil of unity in our families for Your glory.
In Jesus' Name.
Amen.
♥

My Own Thoughts and Prayers

♥

♥

Love Always Finds A Way
♥

Honor everyone...
1 Peter 2:17 ESV

Mother wrote a book about her life when she was in her late 80's. She named it *Love Always Finds a Way*.

In her book she wrote, "As I looked back over my life, I tried to show what love can do. If you love enough, you can do great things."

Some may not deem caregiving as a great thing, but Mother thought it was a way of love. She taught me through her example how to love and care for someone else as I watched her take care of the daily and hourly needs of my sick Grandmother. Mother and Daddy later were caregivers for my Granddaddy and an Uncle. I didn't realize it then, but God was preparing my own heart for the task of caregiver for my mother in her latter days.

Consequently, when our turn came to care for her, I and my siblings found a way with our own unique gifts to honor her with our love.

One of my brothers was a great protector and keeper of Mother's finances; another brother was good at writing sweet letters to Mother and making things for her with his own hands; another brother called each week, sent cards often, and visited; and lastly, another brother visited and did

121

very special things just for Mother. A sister, who was happy and upbeat, knew how to throw a party that really honored Mother; another sister, strong and brave, always cared lovingly for Mother and for me with acts of service and loving gifts; and another sister came often, bearing thoughtful gifts of love just for Mother and helping me with the load.

How thankful I am that Mother blazed the trail of caregiving before us. Her life taught us that love always finds a way.

♥

Thank You, Father, that by love we can
serve one another.
Thank You for equipping each of us with
gifts to bring joy to others.
Show us ways to honor those we love.
In Your dear Son's Name,
the Name of Jesus.
Amen.

♥

My Own Thoughts and Prayers
♥

♥

Ministers of Love

♥

Thou shalt love the LORD thy God with all thy heart, and with all thy soul, and with all thy mind...and...Thou shalt love thy neighbor as thyself.
Matthew 22:37&39

There are some people who are special ministers of love. They love their neighbor as God commands. I would like to mention here a few of the people who ministered to Mother in such a loving way.

Firstly, there was a hairdresser who, during her day off, went to the homes of the elderly and washed and set their hair. What a blessing she was every Tuesday as she faithfully came and brought her hair dryer, curlers, and other hair necessities. Mother loved her, and she loved Mother. When the hairdresser had finished, Mother looked as though she could win first place in a beauty pageant for ladies over ninety years of age. We can never thank her enough for her ministry of love and kindness to Mother.

Secondly, we enjoyed the ministry of our friend and pastor emeritus who came to visit with Mother. He played his fiddle, harmonica, and he blew his famous train whistle. He always prayed and left us encouraged by his prayers and songs.

What a blessing he was to Mother and to us. How grateful we are for our special "Ministers of Love."

Thirdly, there was an anointed singer who soothed our hearts and minds with his quiet, gentle voice as he sang melodies divine. He was invited to celebrate and to sing to us on Mother's Day, her birthdays, a family member's wedding or just a special gathering. What a blessing he was! He never charged for his singing; He truly sings for God's glory.

Fourthly, we had a dear logger friend who sang songs with his Appalachian accent. He wrote many songs about Heaven which he shared with us. Though he had been diagnosed with cancer, he sang to Mother with a gleam in his eye.

♥

Father, we are so grateful for the ministers
of love who freely gave so much of themselves
to us and especially to Mother.
In The Lovely Name of Jesus.
Amen.
♥

My Own Thoughts and Prayers
♥

♥

The Gift of a Burden
♥

Cast thy burden upon the LORD,
and he shall sustain thee...
Psalm 55:22

Whenever I read my Bible now or read a devotional book, I find notations of dates with the word "Mother" written by them. These marked passages of scriptures and poems often spoke to my situation, and they encouraged me to claim God's sustaining power in my life. They helped me to have faith that God had placed this burden into my life for a purpose.

Interestingly though, the Hebrew word for "burden," used here in Psalms 55, actually means "gift." One may ask themselves, "how can a burden be a gift?"

Our burdens are our wings; on them we soar to higher realms of grace; without them we must roam for aye on planes of undeveloped faith, (for faith grows but by exercise in circumstance impossible). Oh, paradox of Heaven. The load we think will crush was sent to lift us up to God!" And "When God puts a burden upon you He puts His own arms underneath...

—Miss Mary Butterfield

The eternal God is your refuge, and his everlasting arms are under you.
Deuteronomy 33:27ESV

129

Blessed is any weight,
however overwhelming,
which God has been so good
as to fasten with His own hand
upon our shoulders.

—*F. W. Faber*

Be still my soul! The Lord is on thy side;
Bear patiently the cross of grief or pain;
Leave to thy God to order and provide;
In every change He faithful will remain.
Be still, my soul! Thy best, thy heavenly Friend
Thro' thorny ways leads to a joyful end.

—*Katharina von Schlegel*

♥

Heavenly Father and Lord of all, calm our
quivering souls bowed down by our load. Help us
accept Your gift of a burden, for it teaches us of
Your wondrous grace and sustaining power. Father,
thank You for the refuge we find in You, in Your
Word, and in devotional books that lift us up to You.
We rest in Your loving arms as You carry us
through the enormous task of caregiving.
In Jesus' Name. Amen.
♥

My Own Thoughts and Prayers
♥

♥

132

His Grace for a Mad Caregiver
♥

If possible, so far as it depends on you,
live peaceably with all.
Romans 12:18 ESV

"Live peacefully with **all**"? I am so glad God said "if possible," because sometimes it is impossible!

I hate to admit it, but we caregivers can get a little "crazy" sometimes. And that means no peace.

The stress can become so intense that we say and do things we would not do under normal circumstances. We may become short-tempered, impatient, irrational, and sometimes very volatile.

Irrationality is what happened one day when one of my sisters came to see Mother. Something was said or done that ignited the time bomb within me. When I asked her and her husband to leave, she refused. I was getting desperate; I needed space and time to recover. I told her if she didn't leave, I would call the police. Talk about irrational: I was it!

Now, doesn't that sound like a godly woman and caregiver? I am ashamed that I got to that point. It was a crude and childish way to react to anyone. But something very simple can push our button, and then, like a volcano, we erupt into something deadly. I felt I could handle no more of whatever it was. I knew that my life was spinning out of control and I needed control somewhere!

Praise God for His grace which He extends to us when it seems impossible to live peacefully with another person. His grace is available to us, though, we may feel so unworthy of it. Meet with Him at His throne room of grace.

♥

Loving Heavenly Father, I am thankful
You are in control, and I can rest in Your
sovereignty. Please forgive me for hurting others.
Let me be calm in the ocean of Your love. You are
with me and love me no matter what. For I am Your
child. Please help me to act like I belong to You,
and bring honor to the name of Jesus.
Amen.
♥

My Own Thoughts and Prayers
♥

♥

The Fabric of Friendship
♥

A friend loveth at all times,
and a brother is born for adversity.
Proverbs 17:17

Like a Mighty Quilter,
The LORD with His own hand,
Has woven us together
In a quilt of friendship grand!
—rgc

What a wonderful gift friendship is to the caregiver. I had some very loyal comrades that came along beside me with prayers, encouragement, and loving help. Some sat and held my mother's hand and encouraged her and me. We had friends who loved to take pictures. What wonderful treasures they gave us, those memories locked in time! Also, there were always friends bearing gifts. I could not have made it without the help and love of my dear friends. Although sisters were also my friends, I all too often didn't realize it or accept them as such.

Dear caregiver, is it hard for you to accept help from others? Please don't think you can do it by yourself. You may think: *why bother any one else with my problems?*

The Bible tells us that...

"Two are better than one; because they
have a good reward for their labor. For if they fall,

137

*the one will lift up his fellow: but woe to him that is
alone when he falleth; for he hath not another to
help him up.*
Ecclesiastes 4:9

It's not a sin to need help. It will be a joyful
opportunity for someone else to help you. Now,
take that hand your friend is stretching out to you
and be blessed!

♥

Thank you, Father, for friends who lay
down their lives for a friend.
That's the kind of friend You are to us.
You laid down Your life so that we might live.
Praise Your Holy Name.
Amen.
♥

My Own Thoughts and Prayer
♥

♥

My Beloved, Come Away With Me!

♥

Then, because so many people were coming and going that they did not even have a chance to eat, He said to them, "Come with me by yourselves to a quiet place and get some rest".
Mark 6:31 NIV

My mother had a phrase for a house full of people and confusion and it is "Grand Central Station." I've traveled recently to Grand Central Station in New York City, and it is indeed busy with people coming and going.

Our home was much like that while Mother was with us. She loved company and the attention she got from them. She loved people. She was a lovely hostess, always was so polite, and tried hard to make each visitor feel more than welcomed to our home.

Although the many visitors drained my energy at times, I am grateful for each one and for what each contributed to Mother's health. However, it did get hectic sometimes.

It was then that I felt the strong need to get by myself in a quiet place with the Lord to allow Him to restore my strength.

You may have a quieter schedule than ours was, but one can get so busy caregiving that we forget to eat, or we neglect the essentials to have good health.

141

When life gets wearisome and hectic for you, remember the words of Jesus: "come with Me and rest a while."

Tarry not for an opportunity to have more time alone with Me. Take it, though ye leave the tasks at hand...Our time together is like a garden full of flowers...

—*Frances Roberts*

♥

Father, thank you for the example Jesus gave us in His Word. Tired and hungry disciples deserved to rest and so do we.
Thank you!
In our Savior's Name, Jesus.
Amen.

♥

My Own Thoughts and Prayers

♥

♥

The Last Christmas

♥

For the Father Himself loveth you,
because ye have loved me, and have believed that I
came out from God.
John 16:27

Mother's health failed rapidly. Her bowels refused to work. She had bronchitis and cried to go home to heaven. My husband, who is a Physician Assistant, kept a close eye on her and an ear to her chest. She stayed in bed, not wanting to get up and also lacking the strength to do it well.

On our last Christmas day with Mother, our daughter, her husband and their six children visited with Mother. Many times Mother would be confused and not know us, but this day she was alert. I asked Mother if she would pray a blessing over our daughter, her family, my husband and me. She readily agreed. We gathered around her bed as she raised her hand to bless us.

"Father, bless my children and keep them in the hollow of Your hand. May they love and serve You all of their days... We ask for Jesus' Sake. Amen."

She always prayed the sweetest prayers thanking God for simple things and for others. I am so glad we asked her to pray for us. We had no idea she would be gone from us so soon. Her blessing rested on each one of us. What a treasured memory for us.

Our son and his family came the next day. She always loved to see the children. She loved her children and grandchildren and she prayed for us often. As her last days crept closer, she prayed aloud for God to take care of her children.

Mother loved poetry from a child. She often quoted poems to anyone who would listen to her. She had a marvelous memory until the last few years of her life.

One of her favorite poems was "A Psalm of Life" by Henry Wadsworth Longfellow. One line in particular is a special reminder to us children, that like Mother, our lives can be sublime for the Lord:

> *...and departing, leave behind us*
> *Footprints on the sands of time.*

♥

Father, thank You for precious memories like these with Mother. Make our foot prints worthy for others to follow.
For Jesus' Sake.
Amen.
♥

My Own Thoughts and Prayers

♥

♥

Rewards of Caregiving

♥

And let us not grow weary in well doing:
for in due season we shall reap,
if we faint not.
Galations 6:9

It had been an extra hard Sunday for Mother and me. With my back tired and achy, I heaved to move her from the edge to the middle of the bed. I prayed silently, "Lord, what is it you want from me through this hardship with Mother?" Mother looked at me and said, "Keep on doing the good work. You are doing a good work." I was shocked! God really answered that prayer in a split second. He sent the encouragement I needed through Mother. What an awesome God!

But little did I know that in less than five weeks Mother would go home to be with the Lord. I didn't realize that my days to tuck my dear Mother into bed were numbered. After Mother was snug in her bed, I quickly wrote in my journal what had transpired. I am so thankful I had penned my feelings and her words.

Dear caregiver, you also are doing a good work. Your sacrificial work has not gone unnoticed by God. He is very aware of it. He is with us all the way. He sends encouragement and strength for both the caregiver and the loved one.

O, for faith to cast behind me every sad
complaint—
Faith to run and not be weary, walk and never faint;
Thou dost know and feel my weakness, Savior look
on me;
Now Thy tender mercy pleading,
let me lean on Thee.

—*Fanny Crosby*

♥

Father, thank You for Your encouragement and
strength to care for our loved ones.
Thank you for answered prayer.
Help us to be faithful to the task at hand
no matter what.
In Jesus' Precious Name.
Amen.
♥

My Own Thoughts and Prayers

♥

♥

The Faithful Servant

♥

His master said to him,
"Well done, good and faithful servant. You have
been faithful over a little; I will set you over much.
Enter into the joy of your master."
Matthew 25:21ESV

Joseph was a faithful servant of the Lord though he was mistreated and put into prison because he was faithful. God had a plan, and he rewarded Joseph's faithfulness. Joseph was lifted up to a position second only to Pharaoh. What joy was his for all the years of toil. Now, that should inspire us all to faithfulness!

We may never have that kind of "lifting up," but God does have in store honor and positions beyond our imagination in the life to come for the faithful caregiver. His angels are watching and taking notes. He knows all our sacrifices, heartaches, and pain.

Nothing goes unnoticed. His blood covers our sins as we confess them, but the good deeds are written down in His books for rewards now and for later.

God has a special place in His heart for the caregiver. So, when He sees your service and obedience to Him, it makes Him smile! His heart is warmed by your sacrifice of service to another that is made in His image.

153

The Father's approving smile is waiting for you at the end of your tunnel, faithful one!

For God is not unfair. He will not forget how hard you have worked for him and how you have shown your love to him by caring for other Christians, as you still do.
Hebrews 6:10 NLT

♥

Thank You, Father,
for the hope that is in You for joy and for good.
Our efforts are not in vain!
In Jesus' Name.
Amen.

♥

My Own Thoughts and Prayers
♥

The Shadow of Death

♥

*Yea, though I walk through the valley of the shadow
of death, I will fear no evil: for Thou art with me...*
Psalm 23:4

"The valley of the shadow of death" that the
Psalm speaks of sounds so dark, lonesome, and
eerie. However, the Lord showed me through a
friend how to view this verse in a different light.
While mother lay dying in the hospital with
pneumonia, a friend, whose husband occupied a bed
down the hall, gently knocked on our door. I quietly
slipped out of the room to see what she needed.

This friend shared with me what she had
learned that morning in her daily devotion from
Psalm twenty-three verse four: "Yea, though I walk
through the valley of the shadow of death..." She
said, "You know, when light is present, it makes a
shadow." The light of that truth slowly dawned on
my weary mind as she spoke, and I understood that
the Light that made the shadow in this verse was the
Lord Jesus, the Good Shepherd, the Light of the
world! What a wonderful revelation! It carried us
through Mother's painful journey through that
valley, for we knew Jesus was with her.

Some may wonder where God is when they
walk with a loved one, or by themselves, through
the valley of the shadow of death. God, our
Emmanuel, stays with us for He has promised never
to leave us, nor to forsake us. We may not see His

157

Light, but we know He is there when we see the shadow of His presence.

And for us who remain after our loved one is gone, we can hide under the shadow of His wings:

How excellent is thy lovingkindness, O God!
therefore the children of men
put their trust under the shadow of Thy wings:
For with Thee is the fountain of life:
in Thy light shall we see light.
Psalm 36:7 & 9

♥

Father, thank you for friends who share Your truths when we need Light for our dark moments. Thank you for being with us in the shadows of our life. We can rest knowing You, our Light, are there. We will fear no evil with You by our side.
In the lovely name of Jesus I pray.
Amen.
♥

My Own Thoughts and Prayers
♥

In My Father's House

♥

*...and I will dwell in the house of
the LORD for ever.*
Psalm 23:6 b

As Mother's spirit left this earth, she was
surrounded by three of her children and their
spouses. We had sung, prayed, read the Word, and
had given constant words of encouragement all
morning to her. Mother's breathing became slower.
My husband, a Physician Assistant, said, "She is
now taking her last few breaths." My sister-in-law
said, "We should have music as she goes." At that
very instant, as she breathed her last breath and
entered the gates of glory, my cell phone rang to the
tune of the "Grand Waltz Brillante." It was an
appropriate song, for we could see mother dancing
her way into glory.

Mother often danced for us when we were
children. She danced the Charleston, and with her
long legs, she could kick higher than her head.
Years later at a family reunion, Mother, pretending
to be dancing and whirling, flared out her full skirt
as my brother caught her performance and graceful
pose on camera. What a treasured picture.

That was our mother, always dramatic and
full of life. Now, her body lay cold and her face was
relaxed and beautiful. Thoughts of her dancing in
heaven filled our minds. She was dancing now, not
to the "Grand Waltz," but to the music the angels
were singing.

What a comfort to know where she was. Apostle Paul writes in II Corinthians 5:8: "We are confident, I say, and willing rather to be absent from the body, and to be present with the Lord."

I hope you know where your loved ones are going and that you will see them again. God gives an invitation to all who will come to His dear Son for salvation.

I hope you will accept His invitation. You will dance for joy in your heart.

♥
Thank You, Father, for the hope
we have in Jesus of seeing our loved ones again in
heaven.
In Jesus' Name.
Amen.
♥

My Own Thoughts and Prayers

♥

♥

Footprints to Follow

♥

... follow after righteousness...
1 Timothy 6:11

Linda Ellis relates to us in her poem, "The Dash," that the most important thing is what we do in the time (dash) between the date of birth and date of death carved on our tombstone.

Mother's days were full of faith, fun, work, adventure, and sadness. She was a teenage bride. She was fifteen and my dad was twenty-four when they married. They ran away in my dad's Model T Ford and were married by a justice of the peace. My grandmother sent the police to arrest her new son-in-law, but when my mother vowed she would go with him to jail, my grandmother dropped the charges.

God blessed Mother and Daddy with nine children. Mother thought that there was always room for one more so they fostered three teenage boys.

Mother, a wonderful and captivating speaker, taught mission study courses in Georgia and at the Ridgecrest Baptist Assembly.

Mother's struggle with cancer followed by the loss of her eldest son, nearly destroyed her. However, her resilient faith in God brought her through, and she served the Lord for many years.

Mother and Daddy volunteered to be Baptist missionaries in Tokyo, Japan. They served as house parents in a dormitory for the missionaries' children. They also traveled around the world together and lived to celebrate their golden wedding anniversary.

Mother was always busy with the King's business on the highway of life, witnessing to both neighbors and strangers of the Savior's love and of His power to save. Mother lived a full life for others a marvelous "dash!"

Her grandson, Bob Kilpatrick, the writer and composer of the song, "In My Life Lord, Be Glorified," also wrote a song about Mother entitled, "Footprints to Follow on the Highway of the King."

♥

Thank You, Father, for Mother's life. Thank You
that we can safely
follow in her footsteps.
In Jesus' Precious Name.
Amen.
♥

166

My Own Thoughts and Prayers
♥

♥

No Regrets
♥

...or whatsoever ye do,
do all for the glory of God
I Corinthians 10: 31

Does anyone truly believe that he can do everything right with no regrets in life? We like to think that we can and will. However, I have not met anyone with a perfect record of never getting angry, never having a pity-party, or never being impatient. Neither have I have ever met anyone who spent all the time with a loved one they should have spent. It just doesn't happen.

What do you do with your regrets? What do you do when you feel defeated? I run to Jesus!

Joseph Hart wrote these words in an old hymn:

I will arise and go to Jesus,
He will embrace me in His arms;
In the arms of my dear Savior,
O there are ten thousand charms.

That's the safest place —in the arms of Jesus when the devil whispers to us, "if only you had done_____." He is the accuser of the Brethren and wants us to feel that we have failed at what God has given us to do.

Don't be discouraged. Joyce Landorf Heatherly offers encouraging words to us in her book *Balcony People* (57) where she wrote:

"Your care for others is the measure of your greatness."

Keep her words in mind. For it is not what you didn't do, but the loving care you did give to your loved one. That is the measure of the greatness of your work.

♥

Father, help us not to listen to the enemy when he
pounds us with thoughts of regret. Enable us to
forgive ourselves for failings and to accept Your
everlasting mercy as we run into your arms.
Let all that we do glorify You.
Thank You that Jesus alone is our Righteousness.
Only He is perfect. Praise His Holy Name.
Amen.

♥

My Own Thoughts and Prayers
♥

♥

The Counsel of His Own Will
♥

In whom also we have obtained an inheritance,
being predestinated according to the purpose of him
who worketh all things after the counsel of his own
will.
Ephesians 1: 11

And we know that all things work together for good
to those who love God, to those who are the called
according to His purpose.
Romans 8:28

How thankful I am that for His children, God works all things out for our good and after the counsel of His own will. He weaves together the circumstances of our lives into a lovely tapestry. Now, when He was sticking me with that giant heavenly needle, I did not enjoy it at all. But when I reflect, I see His hand of mercy.

My husband was a haven for me as I cried on his shoulder. A lot of marriages break up when a spouse becomes a caregiver because of the stress and when needs go unmet. But, it brought us closer together in many ways and separated us in others.

It was not easy for us to carry on a normal marriage. I tried to meet my husband's needs, but truly I felt pulled in two directions many times. You know the feeling your heart is always in two places feeling you need to be with _____, but wanting to stay where you are.

We missed visiting in our children's homes. We seldom went to our grandson's ball games. Or if we did, we needed to rush back quickly after the game. No time for hanging around enjoying our children and grandchildren after the game.

Yes, we missed a lot, but we have the joy and satisfaction of knowing we cared for my elderly mother in our home in obedience to what God had called us to do. We grew and matured through the sacrifices we made.

I know you must feel that you are missing out on many things, but it is part of the sacrifice. Though the time seems like forever when you are going through it, looking back, it is like but a moment in time.

♥

Lord, we rest in Your loving sovereignty.
Help us to make the most of every precious
moment you give us with our loved one.
In Jesus' Name.
Amen.
♥

My Own Thoughts and Prayers
♥

Crossroads

♥

Consider mine affliction,
and deliver me:
for I do not forget Thy Law.
Psalm 119:153

The painful details of my trials are almost too much to recall. The time Mother had to enter the nursing home when my husband and I thought we were moving to the West was especially grievous to me. This was after he lost his job. He was also trying to save me from the difficult task of caregiving. However, after his job interviews in Colorado and New Mexico, we knew that we had to come home and rescue Mother from the nursing home. The pain of Mother being in the nursing home nearly destroyed me physically and emotionally. It was four months before my siblings agreed to let her return to our home.

It was torturous to go each day to see Mother knowing how much she wanted to return home. I felt so guilty and so torn. It took a lot of work for my siblings to acquire a place for Mother into the nursing home. The suggestion of her leaving angered them. I can't blame them. They were trying to help relieve me of the heavy responsibility. They felt I was unable to continue caring for her. And they didn't know if my husband and I would keep our new commitment to care for Mother again. Now, I understand their position completely.

But we were able to do it with God's help, even though I know it hurt my siblings for me to bring mother back home. We were trying to honor my Mother. She wanted to return to my home. She wanted to leave the nursing home. The weight of the burden became the blessing of which Faber speaks. And God gave me the promised strength each day.

By affliction, the Master Artist is adding some new touch of loveliness to the picture He is bringing out in our souls.

— J.R. Miller

♥

Lord, it has been good for me to be afflicted so that
I could learn Your statutes.
In Thy Precious Son's Name, Jesus.
Amen.
♥

My Own Thoughts and Prayers
♥

♥

180

Sisters for Sale!

♥

But Martha was distracted with much serving, and
she approached Him and said, "Lord, do You not
care that my sister has left me to serve alone?
Therefore tell her to help me."
Luke 10: 40 NKJV

There were times while caring for Mother
that I felt like the little child in Michelle Medlock
Adams children's book who wanted to sell his sister.

When I found the book, *Sister for Sale*, at a
writer's conference I thought it sounded like a good
idea. It was just what I had been feeling. So I
purchased the book and savored the thought all the
way home.

I raised the "For Sale" sign in my heart
because I was frustrated and disappointed with my
sisters. I felt like Martha, Lazarus's sister, who had
a problem with her sister. Mary sat at the feet of
Jesus listening to Him instead of helping Martha.

Like Martha, I made my complaint to Jesus,
"Why don't they help me more instead of
_____?"

However, Jesus answered Martha with these
words, which resounded in my own heart:

Martha, Martha, you are worried and
troubled about many things.

181

But one thing is needed and Mary has chosen that good part, which shall not be taken away from her.
Luke 10:41

It was then that God showed me my own deceitful heart.

♥

Lord, if I had been worshipping at Your feet, maybe I would not have been so resentful of them as I served alone. Maybe they would have helped me more. Father, forgive me and help me take down my "For Sale" sign and love them anyway. O, may I never foreget. Lord, Christina Rossetti's words:

For there is no friend like a sister
In calm or stormy weather;...

In our Exalted Brother's Name,
the Name of Jesus.
Amen.
♥

My Own Thoughts and Prayers

♥

Forgiving One Another

♥

And be ye kind one to another, tenderhearted
forgiving one another, even as God for Christ's
sake hath forgiven you.
Ephesians 4:32

I have to admit that this is a hard one for me. But life is too short to hold a grudge or to harbor bitterness in our hearts. To not forgive makes us sick. Why would we want to make ourselves ill?

When Mother had to live in a nursing home, I thought my siblings would never forgive me when Mother insisted that she go back home to live with us. Some wanted her in the nursing home because they knew it was hard for me, but others seemed to want control.

The pain I experienced was horrible. There is nothing like emotional pain, and the guilt was unbearable! It took the bitter struggle with siblings while Mother was in the nursing home for four months to break the bitterness in our family. It is a long story, but God did it through a chain of events.

I am grateful for the peacemaker in our family who set all seven of us straight and would not let anyone blame the other or ourselves. "God did this!" she said. And that was the beginning of healed relationships within my family.

Often, pride will stand in the way of our admitting that we were wrong. It can block our ability to ask for forgiveness when we have hurt someone.

Is there someone today that needs His grace extended to them through you?

♥

Father, keep our hearts clean of bitterness each day so that You will be glorified in our lives. Thank You for Your mercy. Help us to extend Your mercy to others in our relationships. Enable us to forgive each other and ourselves..
For Your glory!
Amen
♥

Nothing Between

Nothing between my soul and the Saviour...
Nothing preventing the least of His favor,
Keep the way clear! Let nothing between.

—C.A.Tindley

My Own Thoughts and Prayers
♥

♥

Let's Run Away!

♥

For the LORD is great, and greatly to be praised;
He is to be feared above all gods.
Psalm 96:4

There was a time when my husband and I decided to leave our desired haven to run away to another state far away from the pain, hurt, and the endless burden. But God would not let us. He had more to do in our lives and in the lives of my siblings. Praise God. I am so thankful that He did not let us leave the task He had given us.

God rewarded us with a miracle of His grace and mercy. We had to put our farm up for sale when my husband lost his job. An investor, who was very gracious, purchased our house and agreed to let us stay for six months. Then a young couple from another state purchased the house and would not be ready to move for several more years. So Mother was able to stay in her room, and my husband found work without us moving away. By God's grace we didn't really lose our miracle farm. We all are just stewards, anyway, of what God puts into our hands. **He** really owns it all.

We are all prone to leave the task at hand, to not finish the race. May He grant us grace to stay with His plan for our life.

Therefore, let us consider this text from the Bible...

189

… let us lay aside every weight,
and the sin which doth so easily beset us, and let us
run with patience the race that is set before us.
Looking unto Jesus the author and finisher of our
faith; who for the joy that was set before Him
endured the cross…
Hebrews 12:1-2

♥

O to grace how great a debtor
Daily I'm constrained to be!
Let Thy goodness, like a fetter,
Bind my wandering heart to Thee.
Prone to wander, Lord, I feel it,
Prone to leave the God I love;
Here's my heart, O take and seal it,
Seal it for Thy courts above.

—*Robert Robinson, 1758*

Amen.
♥

My Own Thoughts and Prayers
♥

♥

Closing Thoughts

♥

*Now the God of hope fill you with all joy and peace
in believing, that ye may abound in hope, through
the power of the
Holy Ghost.
Romans 15:1.*

It is so hard to say good-bye to you. I have tried to imagine your life and what you must be going through as I have shared my experiences with you. You have been in my heart the whole journey through this book. I pray you have found hope in God as you have read my experiences.

He has put a loved one into your life and hands. However, each one of us has to decide what we can and can not do, and leave the rest to God. If the time comes when you can no longer care for your loved one, He is faithful to give you strength to do whatever you must do.

Sometimes it may become necessary for a professional to take over the care of your loved one. Maybe your health has broken down completely, or the stress-related things are just too much for you to carry on. Take all your fears, guilt, questions, and the feeling of being powerless to change things to the Lord and leave them with Him.

Receive the help offered by friends and your church family to support you in your decision. And remember that God smiles down on your life and your sacrifice.

Every time I see one of you out there caring for a parent, child, husband or wife who is unable to care for themselves, my heart warms in the radiance of your life. It always makes me think of Mother when I see you, and I feel close to her again. I love you!

♥

Father, thank You for allowing me to share my caregiving journey with other caregivers. Bless them and strengthen them each day for the task you have given them. Be honored and glorified in their service to You and their loved one.
For Jesus' Sake.
Amen.

♥

P. S.
I'd love to hear from you.
You may email me at
hisgrace4amadcaregiver@windstream.net

Credits

The Crucible

Poem "I Wonder" by Ruth Harms Calkin used by permission.

A Grateful Heart

Copyright Revive Our Hearts/ Taken from Nancy Leigh DeMoss' Choosing Gratitude; Used With permission.
www.ReviveOurHearts.com.

The Great Escape

Quotes from Jim Elliot's diary are taken from a copy of a personal letter from Elizabeth Elliot in Shandia, Ecuador, January 25, 1956 to her friends. Used by permission.

The Gift of a Burden

Miss Mary Butterfield's poem, taken from *Streams In the Desert* compiled by Mrs. Chas. E. Cowman, pages 76-77 Copyright 1950 (Cowman Publications, Inc.)

When Wounds Become Windows

Song entitled, "When Wounds Become Windows" by Bob Kilpatrick. Used by permission.

The Gift of a Burden

Psalm 55 in: "The Gift of a Burden" The Defender's Study Bible, Henry M. Morris PhD., LLD, Lih; Page 872.

No Regrets

Quote in No Regrets is from *Balcony People* by Joyce Landorf Heatherly, page 57. Used by permission.

My Beloved, Come Away With Me

Frances Roberts, *Come Away My Beloved* (Voice Publications, Northridge, California, 1969), 13.

♥

A special
"Thank you",
To
Mr. and Mrs.
Lewis Schoettle
for your meticulous care in
publishing this lovely book.
May God bless you
abundantly!

♥

Love,
Rebecca